A Gift of Love to Myself

Pain and Blessings of Love

By: Porchea Harlan

"A Gift of Love to Myself
Pain and Blessings of Love" copyrighted by
Porchea Harlan. 2024 All Rights Reserved.

All rights reserved. No part of this publication may be reproduced, distributed, or transmitted in any form by any means, including photocopying, recording, or other electronic methods without the prior written permission of the author, except in the case of brief quotations embodied in reviews and certain other noncommercial uses permitted by copyright law. For permission requests, write to the author.

Printed in United States of America
First Edition: 2024
ISBN: 9798879541809
Written By: Porchea Harlan

Dedication to my daughter Kamari

I never knew what unconditional love was until the tender age of 19. I gave birth to my first child. I labored for about 13 hours on Valentine's Day. It was painful. I was scared and worried about whether I was worthy of such an amazing gift from God. My precious daughter saved my life. At that moment I knew childhood trauma was no longer my Achilles heel. Within seconds of giving birth to her my mom whispered in my ear and asked me if there was something I wanted to tell her. Because my baby was so light skinned when she was born my mother questioned if I had told the truth about who her father was.

As I laid there fighting for my life and my newborn daughter these were the words my mother had whispered to me. I had dilated from 6cm to 10cm in 15 minutes or so. No one believed me because it was my first baby, and I was so young. When my baby was born, she wasn't crying and the umbilical cord was wrapped around her neck twice and around her arm. I had to hold her in my pelvis and not push as the doctor struggled to get the cord from around her neck. She tore me so bad I had 22 sutures to close my body back up. I couldn't hold her immediately because the resuscitation team had to examine her.

And before I knew if my baby was ok this is what was whispered in my ear prior to holding my baby. I remember laying in pain while the doctor was suturing me to stop me from hemorrhaging and asking why my baby wasn't crying. Completely unconcerned about my own life and the pain I was enduring, my concern in that moment was her and her life that had just begun.

Dedication to my daughter Kamryn

To my sweet daughter, Kamryn I thank God every day for you. You have been the greatest miracle, lesson and blessing of my life. You're my angel. God trusted me to take care of you, something so precious. I am honored to be your mother. And I will always always always have your back. Forever mines and I'm forever yours.

Love, Mom

A letter from my mother

To my daughter Porchea

What is a daughter? The online dictionary defines a daughter as a direct descendant or offspring of their parents. In a simpler word, a daughter is a beautiful extension of their mother and a beautiful gift from God. That's what you are to me Porchea.

No words can truly express what you mean to me, other than to say with great honor you are my daughter, who I am so incredibly proud of and I am so honored to be your mother.

I have much respect for you as a woman and admire the woman that you have become. I love everything about you, your resilience, how you bounce back when they think you're down, your giving heart, your generosity is amazing, and your sense of style is impressive. You're a bad chick, so smart and because of the two parents you have, nutty as a fruit cake, a woman who knows how to stand up for herself, right or wrong.

Best of all, I love the wonderful mother that you have become, and I am so thankful for beautiful granddaughters that you have given to me, including the fact that the same strength and character I tried so hard to put in you, I see you are putting the same effort into your own daughters.

Proving to the world that a daughter is an offspring and or beautiful extension of their mother.

To my daughter,
From your mom

My ultimate spouse

He can make me laugh
Tall, dark and handsome
Has a beard
Makes good money
Ambitious
Confident
Makes me feel safe and secure
Not more than five years older or younger than me
College-educated
Knows how to satisfy me in the bedroom
Appreciates my daughters, aka good father
Knows how to handle my mama
Enjoys the simple things in life like my home cooking, cuddling, and watching movies
Knows how to be a leader of our family.

Sometimes forever isn't always forever...

Today, the new love that I thought was so rare became all too familiar. Do I wait for love or escape this love? How could this be love? I guess forever isn't always forever. My love and his love were supposed to be that forever kinda love but now this love will forever be a never ever love.

Hurt, pain, frustration, and all the emotions in between can't explain this forever, and that will never be. Obstacles before the peak of our love now stand in the way of our forever. Before it could be spoken, his eyes today told me our forever was no longer.

My brother's keeper

It really hit home today. I never knew how much he needed me to have his back before today. I won't lie; I let the frustration of his nonverbal love for me stiffen my regard for him.

I always wondered why he and everyone else thought I was so strong. But it was because he needed me to be. We share a bond that the others don't.

He and are kindred spirits. Always so vocal, the life of the party, people are attracted to our charismatic personalities.

Though our 23 pairs come from the same source, it is not this alone that we subconsciously are bonded through. It's the overwhelming feeling of Loneliness is the thought of knowing one else truly understanding us. The gift of looking so well put together but scattered on the inside.

For as long as I could remember, I've instinctively felt the need to defend and protect him. I still remember tying his shoes and trying to open up a can of whoop ass on the playground.

Why was this instinct so strong, and why was it never reciprocated from him to me? Why was I tasked with being my brother's keeper?

One day, he revealed that I was the closest thing to him. Though it was always there, it became a burden that guilted me over the years because I never felt like he loved me the way I loved him.

But it's the kindred spirit that I know we share that will never let me turn my back on him, for I am my brother's keeper. Life is about the journey with a destination unknown. As you navigate the twists and turns, the inevitable happens, and your destiny unfolds. Destiny or destination are they not the same, or does one determine the other?

Was it love, or was it lust... From the beginning he parted, he filled my brain with intellectual passion. The way his tailored suit clanged to his body evicted every ounce of restraint from my mind.

He had this charismatic energy that I wanted him to share with me in the most intimate way. When we first met, the world around us was full of fear and uncertainty. I believe it was this fear that intertwined our bodies and created an orgasmic energy of hope.

The sacredness of our interaction was formed out of the unknown. It was the thought and hope of what we could be that cradled and sheltered our minds from the pandemic around us.
We were embarking on uncharted territory with each other and the world around us, but our hearts connected in ways that felt nostalgic.

Laying in his arms for the first time, sharing my most sacred and hurtful memories came organically. When I cried, he kissed my forehead, nose, and cheek in the most sincere way. How could this not be love?

His situation was not perfect, though, and neither was mine. My heart had been broken too many times,, and he seemed to be exhausted. One day, he said I kept trying to give him conditional love because I was not his only one. It was in that moment that I knew I could not walk away. So, I tried my best to stay in the moment with him and let every moment be enough.

Maybe he would not be mine always,, and maybe he would, but I will always be grateful for the moments in time that we shared. We will always be bonded by the historic and fearful events in life and the world by an intimacy only known to us.

Porchea in a Porsche takes Vegas.

Him checking out my rear end.
We held hands the entire time.
He claimed me as his at all times. Grabbed my hand and led around. Opening doors, ushering me in at the hip with his hand
The music he played while he kissed my face.

To have something you never had, you gotta do something you never did…

Men always seem to have the upper hand.
So seemingly that it cripples them.
He won't defeat me.
 Challenge accepted

Depression and anxiety where the fuck did you come from, and why did you pick me?

Most days, I struggle to get out of bed.
I feel tired all the time.
Time is deceiving me.
Every day, a new day begins before I even mastered the day before.
My mind races all the time.
Do you know what it's like to suffocate?
Hopefully you don't, but that's what this illness feels like everyday.
I smile and don't talk about it because people have their own freaking problems.
I have a flight to catch tomorrow
Like why am I even up writing this? Here's a clue because:
insomnia comes with depression and anxiety.

Moments in time of pain love

Hookah and Pinot Grigio.
All that I have left of you.
One of the last things you asked me was if I had been taking my meds.
Human suffering.

Recycling niggas
Misunderstood

He sang to my soul like he was on a rhythm and a beat. Damn microphone piece he used lashed me with lyrics and entangled my spirit with his. All I could think was, damn, his playlist matched mine. Fuck could this be a sign!
Oh hell naw and he fine…. Please, please, please don't turn me into a feen

Stolen memories.

Sex, Love And Lies-

Twisted love
Inconsistent moments
LOVE...
Fake
Superficial moments with hidden intent
LOVE....
What do you know about love?
No pressure, organic vibes, affection, patient.

-Author- Maserati P

You can be vulnerable…

Dedication towards becoming the best version of myself has been my biggest flex so far…

You're only out for self!

That's why you can keep a man!
You're hard to commit too!
Your mentality fucked!
You violated me!
I don't trust you!
I'm not yours!
We not in a relationship or working towards one!
That's why every man that's dealt with you did what he wanted on the side, too!
Your judgment, not shits!
You just gone force me to be tied down to you for life by having this baby!
You not good enough to be my woman!
You need a ward robe makeover!
I deal with women that got more money than you and look better than you all the time!
It ain't supposed to be love!

The higher you get, the harder it gets.

I have truly come to realize that all of my adult experiences, or should I say past experiences, have really molded and shaped me into the woman that I am today and the life that I currently live today.

I'm finally starting to realize that living as my true self and being honest with the people that come into my life is really the best flicks you will ever master in life. Being open and honest about who I am with myself first and foremost and then allow that person to be open and honest with people that come into my life has truly made my life a lot easier

It's also truly allowed me to experience some of the best of other people because I know now that the people that truly choose to be around me and, in my life, I only care because they know who I am and what I'm truly about.

Call me crazy, but it's something super sweet about this man calling me and falling asleep on the phone.

Can I look?
He's still in his truck R&B playing on the radio.
He could be anywhere…

Whenever I'm alone with my thoughts for too long, I become anxious. Feelings of guilt consume me. Lord, please deliver me from the anxiety and pain.

I'm carrying weight that doesn't belong to me. I'll never truly understand the weight of the decisions you had to make to support us, but as a mother myself, all I can say is that I'll do whatever I have to take care of mine.

Will the world ridicule me or celebrate me by being my natural organic self?

When you truly do life with someone, when you truly make a commitment, what it truly means to travel through hail, sleet, or snow, what it truly means to say till death do us part that type of love from last night.

Please don't let it be last night. Our love story had a nasty final.

I think I've found my perfect man. The man God designed just for me. He was my third love.

Whenever I'm with him, I'm in my most creative energy.

I realize now that he is one of my love languages. In my sexuality, my bossiness, my creativity, and my vulnerabilities.

He was my Therapist. Whenever I needed an escape from my reality he was there. Physical time was never our issue. We made time to see each other. We just had to get on each other's schedule.

Thinking of ways to keep this vibe going. He creates that safe space for me.

I can love him wholeheartedly with confidence… I know he won't break my heart.

Catching looks of him right now as I write this. We are so comfortable in each other's space.

Running away from heartache every day is starting to take a toll on me.

I feel like I'm not myself. Being a people pleaser just to survive.

The intensity of those lonely nights takes my breath away sometimes.

I think about the ones that I love. And the ones I thought loved me back.

The purity of love in my heart has been tortured and battered.

Damaged from the moment of conception.
I've tried to shake it, but…

Childhood trauma keeps taunting me

When you elevate your life and mindset but don't elevate the people around you, it's one of the most isolating and loneliest places to be.

Wanted to be a freak for you, wanted to be your everything, I wanted to mean the world to you, I wanted to get money with you, I would've birthed a child for you, but now it's like I don't mean shit to you.

Dear black man.

Normalize seeing the resiliency in your black queens as strength and beauty and not damage. Learn to be patient with her as she has been to you.

Yes, she has loved a man who had not found himself yet, but now, because of her strength, love, and patience, he is ready to stand in the face of a country that has labeled him not a man and say yes, I am.

Yes, she has bore children with a man who lacked the tools to help her raise them, but she raised them, and now they are doctors, lawyers, and entrepreneurs and helping change the view of our people.

Yes, she has been vulnerable in life
because the systematic oppression of our black people has left our black kings murdered, bruised, and beaten for several
generations and unavailable to protect her.

Black men in history have lost their lives for appreciating the beauty of a white woman. How many times has a white man lost his life for appreciating the beauty of a black woman?

How dare you see the pain and scars on her heart and label her damaged. How dare you tell her at any age it's too late for her to focus on your kids because you've spent too much time loving a black man who didn't have the resiliency or guidance to overcome generational curses.

Normalize seeing the strength and beauty in a black woman who has successfully fought through adversity and is still standing with an open heart willing to take a chance yet again on loving a black man.

Normalize seeing a black woman with good credit, good income, a nice home, education, and her own business as a win for our culture instead of labeling her as too independent.

Not a Woman

Through your eyes,, I am not a woman. You say my touch has soothed you and congratulated you. This voice has calmed your anxiety; these ears have listened, and these eyes believe your vision. I am not a woman; you say no kind of woman you lashed once more. My breasts you've caressed, and my thighs you've parted, period. My femininity was there, didn't you feel it? My wound briefly carried your child. But I am not a woman, you say. I saw it in your eyes many times, and I felt in your exhale from the comfort of my embrace the vulnerability of my love, my heart, my mind, my sexiness. My femininity was there, then you feel it. So, OK, most of the pain I endured from our romance was self-inflicted, and I thought it was a form of submission. Tell me, even then, didn't you see it? No, not a woman?

Solitude an undisturbed era. The state or situation of being alone. A lonely or uninhibited place and an essential component to your health and well-being. Being alone versus feeling lonely, they are not the same.

Learning to be comfortable with people constantly staring at me or,, wanting to talk to me, or wanting to know what I'm doing.

"Porchea, you always look so serious, like you're taking care of business". I'm really just lost in my thoughts. I'm trying to figure it out. I'm trying to figure me out. I'm minding my own business. Why can't you? Most days, I'm unaware of the light God has shed on me. The days go by so fast, and I take for granted how constant god's love for me has been. Sometimes I feel burdened with my strength and my ability to be so resilient. I know that he wants to use me to inspire others and spread the message of his love for us, but I've grown weary and tired even though, not of sharing his love but of sharing my testimony.

Every time I felt like my life was swallowing me whole, I was going through transitional moments in my life.

Career goals, mom goals, and relationship goals were crushing me. OMG, the way my hair responded. My self-esteem would be in the trash. Irrational thoughts filled my head, and the heart, consumed me. These thoughts superseded embarrassing and so shocking actions.

I thought I was in love with you. I thought it was safe to love you.

You reminded me that I didn't know what love was. Most importantly, your words and actions prove that I didn't love myself. On days that I struggle with my thoughts of missing you, I go to our text to read the last message you sent to me. I'm thankful that when those words came through, I wasn't alone. It was some of the most awful words ever written to me. Our once sacred soul tie I held on to so tight was now broken beyond repair period. I wanted to hate you, and I hope that one day, you will feel the way your words made me feel. But then I prayed, and God's love for me brought clarity to me. He was using you to shift my focus back to him and my true purpose in life. "Why would I be with a woman that doesn't know how to choose herself?"
 Though my soul was crushed reading the words you wrote me, I thank you. Thank you for being the vessel God used to restore my faith in him and his everlasting love for me.

Minimal spaces being in limbo in between a rock and a hard place, anxiousness is extremely frustrating, leaves a lot for interpretation, room for growth, and a chance to plant seeds.

Embracing softness and realizing that sometimes life is messy. Allow grace and patience with self. Being able to create something when you're in a transitional space is true innovation.

He asked why I always crave companionship.

I fought some of my hardest battles when I was alone period to share time and space, to breathe together and laugh together feels familiar. When I'm alone in my thoughts, I'm afraid. The silence, but loneliness only I can hear. It's unsettling and unnerving. I need someone near. And I wish you were here.

A beautiful mess.

An array of emotions and feelings pour out of me most days. It's hard to fight the current of my soul. I'm a beautiful mess most days. Can others see it too? When I stare back at my reflection I see beauty, I see resilience, I see strength. Still, I'm a beautiful mess most days. This smile, this laugh, my touch, and my song all beat to a rhythm unknown period. Some days, I gained control, but still. I'm a beautiful mess most days.

Pain, why do you chase me, following me into eternity unseemly?

Perhaps it was me chasing you. This feeling is too familiar, it could be the reason I seek you or invite you. Sometimes, it seems purposeful and useful. My successes are parallel in life with my failures. I'll take the lows as long as I get to keep the highs.

Silent tears shut when no one is watching.

Many see me as a machine, and they stare at me in awe and amazement as if what I do is so unimaginable. The OMG and you're crazy, and how do you do what you do weigh heavy on my spirit. Why? Because I've been programmed from birth to always do what I have to do and never give up, but there are many times when I feel like giving up. So, I cry silent tears when I think no one is watching. I don't like being a victim of my circumstances. I don't like to share my story too often because it seems to make people uncomfortable, period. This could be due to the audience I'm generally around. Statistically, I shouldn't have attained the level of success that I have, period the battles I fought internally and externally were strong enough to make anyone, but God fall to their knees and surrender. I don't know how to surrender, even on my worst days. Laying down.

As always, the what ifs and what it could be that caused me to fail every time period, I have to stop bidding my life like a space game three, and a possible is ******* up my grind. Got to take everyone and everything at face value. Pain is like a river. Sometimes, it's calm and gently flows. Other times, the current is so strong it will take you under.

Heartbreaks, breaks heart, heartbroken and broken-hearted.

Why are you here again? I thought I said goodbye to you. You're so familiar that I'm coping better when you are near. Never far away and ever so constant, I yearn for your touch because without it I've never seen. Pain and blessings are both my stories; I never experienced them separately. Broken-hearted but not forever broken. When joy is near or, hold on tight because like Thunder follows lightning joy is the predecessor of my pain. The joy is like a transplant from my broken heart. Today, broken but forever, no, I'm not.

Childhood memories surface, but I don't have fond memories. Pain pain goes away and comes again another day. Today, I'm weak. I can't fight with you this day, like your lullabies and fairy tales.

Sweet tunes to the beat of my tears sound off in my mind, try not to be crippled by my fears.

Truly stay locked in with the people that you love.

Make sure that you are always available to them in some type of way, even if it's just by phone call. If you have to switch up and change your phone number, make sure to give it to certain people in your life. Anytime a person goes completely missing out on your life, make them stand on that shit. And let ************* go *** **** it because chances are they don't really love you; they may mean no harm to you, but they also may not need any good to you. If you say you're out then you gotta also make sure people understand it is a *** **** privilege to be a part of my life *****.

My love letter to him.

I have finally found the love of my life. He was going to love me forever. I never want this love life to end period. I have fallen in love for myself through the eyes of others. I was finally discovering who i was. What's he going to be the stedman of our generation. Because I was for damn sure the new Oprah. He was a real hustler. I could truly love him wholeheartedly. The universe was aligning perfectly for our love to grow. I have decided to have my way. Will he win my heart in the end? I hope he forgives me.

Whenever I'm alone with my thoughts for too long I become anxious.

Feelings of guilt consume me. Lord, please deliver me from this anxiety and pain. I'm carrying weight that doesn't belong to me. I'll never truly understand the weight of the decisions you had to make to support us, but as a mother myself, all I can say is that I'll do whatever I have to take care of mine.

The world was now going to be influenced.

The world was not going to live and breathe off of every word that I spoke, everything that I was wearing, that I ate, and everyone who I love and care for in my life. The world was going to watch me. I was going to write my history, and I was going to become a part of history. I was going to be the new Kerry Washington of my culture; I was going to be the Oprah of my current culture; I was going to be the Megan Good of my current culture; I was going to become the sex symbol of my current age group that reminded men of all those other women I remember a man once telling me that I had to make good vibes. I remember a moment when two people were making jokes about me being Olivia Pope.

I remember my mom referring to me as a model and of women that she thought looked at me or looked like me, similar to the famous actresses. And I almost remember kind of being who is the popular sweetheart, the Lori Harvey of my age group, you know, they talk about Laurie Harvey. And how she moves on from man to man, but this young lady has like that, and now she's reaping the benefit.

And now she's out her dating with the lessons that she learned as a young girl. Don't settle at the end of the day, find a man that is going to fill your life in every way imaginable the way god loves you. Find a man that is going to love you the way god loves you. And there's nothing wrong with it, and when you find that person, when you truly find your person, it is easy and organically so easy that you can just pour it back into that person in a way that's going to be just organic like this is your person and you're their person.

I wanted to be a freak for you, wanted to be your everything, I wanted to mean the world to you, I wanted to get money with you, I would have worn a child for you. But now it's like I don't mean **** to you.

Running away from heartache every day is starting to take a toll on me. I feel like I'm not myself. Being a people pleaser just to survive.

Tonight, I'm seeing a different side of him. He wants me out of my emotions. Tonight, I'm getting clean vibes. He wants me to get lit with him as long as I was being productive with my time and focus on getting to know that I could be anywhere beside him.

My pandemic love story, all three in some way knew of or about each other period book, movie.

I was a part of history. I could help write the history books and moments in time. For black men, playing the video game is therapy. Sports, pleasure whenever I'm with him I'm in my most creative energy. I realize now that he is one of my love languages. And my sexuality, and my bossiness, and my creative impossibilities. He was my therapy period. Whenever I needed an escape from my reality, he was there. Physical time was never our issue. We made time to see each other, period. We just had to get on each other's schedule.

They love me through my music and sex therapy period, and each of them challenges me intellectually.

The three of them are my love language. I desire and cling to a certain piece of each of them. The problem is man #3 could very well be my favorite love, and I don't want to hurt him. The others have already stood ten toes down for me. I'm not sure if he will. If I reveal my truth, will he leave me? The only one that doesn't leave gets to stay, but my way, period. All three mama's boys, so is my brother and father.

The intensity of those long nights takes my breath away sometimes.

I think about the ones that I love. And the ones I thought loved me back. The purity of my love and my heart has been tortured and battered. Damage from the moment of conception. I have tried to shake it, but period... Childhood trauma keeps taunting me.

Made in the USA
Columbia, SC
11 April 2024